Introduction

The push for healthy eating has never been stronger, and this is taking on many forms. Though it used to be something unusual, becoming a vegetarian is one such popular method of eating healthier and cleaner food. There are a lot of misconceptions out there about what it means to eat as a vegetarian, and this cookbook can help to show just how delicious it really can be.

Though there used to be limited options for the vegetarian, that has changed and there is so much more out there. This cookbook will take you through several categories and show you just how simple and delicious eating in this way can really be. It will require you to try new things, but you will love the transition.

Eating as a vegetarian you will learn to embrace how great these foods can make you feel. The foods used within this cookbook are great options for healthier and more balanced eating. The recipes are simple to follow and yet so very effective at providing nutritious, well-rounded, scrumptious meals.

So if you are ready to embrace vegetarian eating, this is the cookbook to help you to get to where you want to be. These recipes offer a wide range of meal options for different tastes. They are easy to follow and before you know it, you will see just how wonderful vegetarian cooking and eating can really be.

Artichoke Soup

Ingredients needed include:

1 lb. each of artichokes and potatoes

1 Spanish onion

1 oz. of butter

1 pint of milk

and pepper and salt to taste.

You are going to wash, peel, and cut the potatoes, artichokes, and onion. Combining them you want to cool them in 1 quart of water, butter, and simple seasoning until they are tender.

Once tender, run them through a sieve and obtain liquid. Take this liquid back to saucepan and add milk, bringing to a boil.

Add water if soup turns out too thick. Add salt and pepper if necessary to season.

Cabbage Soup

1 fair-sized cabbage

a large Spanish onion

1-1/2 oz. of butter

pepper and salt to taste

½ saltspoonful of nutmeg,

1-1/2 pints of milk

2 tablespoonfuls of fine wheatmeal.

Wash the cabbage and then shred up very fine. Then chop up the onion, and set the cabbage and onion aside in a saucepan with 1 quart of water on a medium heat.

Add the butter and seasoning, and let all of the ingredients mix and cook together for about an hour. Stop before the vegetables get too tender.

Add milk and thicken, now cooking until the vegetables are tender. Let this mixture simmer on a lower heat for about 10 minutes.

Once cooked, serve with toasted bread or pita for a nice complement.

Carrot Soup

4 good-sized carrots

1 small head of celery

1 fair-sized onion

1 turnip

3 oz. of breadcrumbs

1-1/2 oz. of butter

1 blade of mace

pepper and salt to taste

Wash the vegetables and carefully scrub them, peeling the carrots. Then chop all of the vegetables and set them over a medium heat combining with water, butter, bread, and mace.

Let the ingredients mix and boil until the vegetables are tender, then run them through a sieve to drain the liquid.

Return the liquid mixture to the saucepan and then season with salt and pepper.

If too thick then add water to the soup, as it should be a cream like consistency.

Potato Soup

2 lbs. of potatoes

½ stick of celery or the outer stalks of a head of celery, saving the heart for table use

1 large Spanish onion

1 pint of milk

1 oz. of butter

a heaped up tablespoonful of finely chopped parsley

pepper and salt to taste

Begin by washing, peeling, and cutting potatoes into small pieces.

Roughly chop the onion, and then cut celery into small pieces as well.

Cook all of the vegetables together in about three pints of water until they are soft. Then run them through a sieve to drain the liquid out.

Return this liquid mixture into the saucepan and then add milk, butter, and seasoning.

Boil the soup again to properly mix all of the ingredients together. Then add water if too thick.

Top with parsley for a garnishment just before serving.

Tomato Soup

1-1/2 lbs. of tomatoes or a large can of tomatoes

1 oz. of butter

3 pints of water (only 2 if canned tomatoes are used)

2 oz. of rice

1 large onion

1 teaspoonful of herbs, pepper and salt to taste

Finely chop the tomatoes and then finely chop the onions as well.

Let the tomatoes and onions cook together in water for about 20 minutes. Then strain the mixture and return the liquid into the saucepan.

Add the remaining ingredients once mixture is in saucepan, and season as needed.

Let the soup cook on a low heat until the rice is tender, and then serve while hot.

Cauliflower Pie

1 small cauliflower

¾ lb. of potatoes

½ lb. of fine wheatmeal

3 eggs

¾ pint of milk

1 oz. of butter

1 saltspoonful of nutmeg, pepper and salt.

Wash and chop the cauliflower and potatoes into small pieces. Then let the two parboil together.

Then take both the cauliflower and potatoes and place into a pie dish with butter and seasoning.

Make a batter out of the meal, milk, and the eggs that you beat beforehand. Pour this batter over the vegetables and then mix everything together well.

Bake at 350 for about 1.5 hours until golden brown.

Celery Croquettes

1 or 2 heads of celery

A teacupful of dried and sifted breadcrumbs

2 eggs

Pepper and salt to taste

Wash the celery and remove the outer stalks. Then steam the parts remaining until they are tender as the basis for this dish.

Cut these pieces into about 2 inch long strips and then dip them into the beaten egg mixture, then into the breadcrumbs to coat.

Then fry the coated celery in bo8ling butter or olive oil until they are a nice golden brown. Dust with salt and pepper for extra seasoning.

Serve up hot right after cooking with tomato sauce on the side for dipping if you wish.

Favorite Pie

3 oz. of macaroni

2 breakfast cupfuls of breadcrumbs

2 onions, chopped very fine

2 breakfast cupfuls of tinned tomatoes

3 eggs, well beaten

3 oz. of butter

1 dessertspoonful of curry, salt to taste

Start by boiling the macaroni until tender, and then once cooled, cut it into about 1 inch long pieces.

Sauté the onion until brown in the butter. Then mix in the breadcrumbs with the tomatoes. Add eggs, curry, onion, and salt, and mix this all together with the chopped macaroni.

Take this complete mixture and put into a pie dish, ensuring it's evenly spread throughout.

Bake this mixture at 350 for about an hour until golden brown. Serve hot and enjoy!

Lentil Turnovers

6 oz. of lentils

6 oz. of mushrooms

1 English onion chopped very fine

1 ounce of butter

1 dessertspoonful of lemon juice, pepper and salt to taste

Separate and wash the lentils carefully, and then cook them in enough water to make them tender but not so much that they soak it all up.

Wash, peel, and chop the mushrooms, and then finely chop the onion. Then combine the two together and sauté them both in the butter until they are tender.

Add the mushrooms and onions to the lentils as they are cooking. Just after add in the lemon juice and the seasoning to this mixture and let it all combine and cook together.

When the lentils are finally soft, take the entire mixture and form into a firm puree.

Let it all cool once in puree. At the same time make a paste of 6 oz. of fine wheatmeal and 2 oz. of butter, along with a little bit of water to hold it all together.

Roll this paste out thin and then cut into squares that are roughly about 4 inches in size.

Take some of the lentil mix and place into each of the formed squares, and moisten the end of each square after doing so.

Turn the square over so that it is in half, and then press the edges together firmly.Bake the turnovers for about 15 minutes in a floured tin at 350.

Serve with a simple sauce and vegetables or potatoes for a nice complement.

Mushroom Tart and Gravy

1 lb. of mushrooms

½ lb. of fine wheatmeal

4 oz. of butter or frying oil

pepper and salt to taste.

Wash the mushrooms thoroughly and then remove the stalks. Then dry them well and cut into small pieces, almost dicing them if you can.

After you set mushrooms aside, start to prepare the pastry crust with the meal and about 3 ounces of butter. Add a fair amount of salt and pepper as these cook together. Then cut the remaining butter into small pieces to mix into the mushrooms for an even coating as this cooks.

Keep a little of the pastry crust paste aside and cut up into thin strips. These will then be placed over the assembled pie after the mushrooms are cooked. You want to create a diamond shape with these extra strips of the meal.

Bake the pie for about 45 minutes at 350 degrees.

To make the gravy:

The stalks of the mushrooms

4 eschalots chopped very fine

1 teaspoonful of cornflour

3 bay leaves

½ oz. of butter

pepper and salt to taste.

Take the stalks of the mushrooms that you previously put aside and toss with the eschalots. Then place this mixture into the butter.

Cook the two ingredients in the butter until tender. Then add in ¾ pint of water and cook all together for about 30 minutes.

Add the seasoning and the bay leaves and let them cook in to add the proper seasoning to the mix. Strain the entire mixture and then return to the pan.

Quickly add in cornflour to thicken the mixture and create the gravy texture that you are looking for. Serve atop the tart and on the side for extra flavor.

Potato and Tomato Pie

2 lbs. of potatoes

2 lbs. of tomatoes

3 hard-boiled eggs

1 oz. of vermicelli or sago

1 Spanish onion

1 dessertspoonful of thyme

1 oz. of butter

pepper and salt to taste

For the crust—

½ lb. of fine wheatmeal

3 oz. of butter

as much cold water as needed to blend together and make a good crust

Take the potatoes and put into a gentle boil in their skins, letting them cook almost through.

When the potatoes are soft, then take them out of water and let them cool. Then cut the potatoes into small pieces and put aside.

Heat the tomatoes and then remove skin carefully. Then when cooled down, cut them into small pieces and combine with potatoes.

Put the potato and tomato mixture into a pie dish and let sit.

Dice the onion finely and then boil in about 1 pint of water. Ad the butter and the vermicelli or sago and let the ingredients cook together. Cook until vermicelli and onion are soft.

Add salt and pepper, and then mix in with potato and tomato mixture until well combined.

Mix all ingredients well and gently mix in thyme for seasoning.

Chop the hard boiled eggs into quarters and then place these pieces over the top of the vegetable mixture.

Make the crust separately and then cover the entire vegetable and egg dish with it.

Bake the pie for about 45 minutes to an hour depending on your oven, usually at about 350 degrees.

Bake until the crust is golden brown. You can get an even golder look to the crust if you brush it with egg white before baking.

Savory Fritters

1 teacupful of mashed potatoes

½ lb. of breadcrumbs

1 large English onion

2 eggs

1 oz. of butter

1 teaspoonful of powdered sage

½ saltspoonful of nutmeg

pepper and salt to taste

Finely chop up the onion and mix in with butter, sautéing until golden brown.

Beat the eggs and then mix these and the onions with the breadcrumbs until combined well.

Then add in the mashed potatoes, herbs, and salt and pepper for seasoning. Mix these all well together with the other ingredients until well blended.

Form this mixture into friggers and then coat in flour.

Fry the fritters up to a golden brown color and let cool slightly before serving.

Spanish Stew

2 lbs. of potatoes

1 lb. of Spanish onions

1 lb. of tomatoes

2 oz. of vermicelli

½ pint of milk

1 oz. of butter

pepper and salt

Finely chop the potatoes and onions and then let them cook in the butter with little or no water. Cook the mixture until it is tender.

Then add in the tomatoes into thin slices. Add to the potato and onion mixture and cook all together for about another 10 minutes or so.

Add in the seasoning, the milk, and the vermicelli to make one larger mixture. Then add a bit more water if necessary so that the mixture doesn't dry out.

Let all of the ingredients cook together for about another 10 minutes or until warm and blended well. Serve hot.

Tomato Tortilla

1 lb. of tomatoes

1 oz. of butter

4 eggs

pepper and salt to taste

Wash tomatoes and then scald them in hot water. Then skin them when slightly cooled. Slice up the skinned tomatoes and set aside.

Melt the butter and then add in the tomatoes with seasoning. Cook the tomatoes in the butter until they are tender. Try to cook until most of the liquid is absorbed by the tomato mixture.

Beat the eggs and then add into the cooked tomatoes. The mixture will thicken as it cooks together, but be sure to mix often.

You can set the mixture aside and chill to use on sandwiches. You can also serve it hot on bread or hot toast for a great meal.

Vegetable Pie

½ lb. each of carrots, turnips, onions, potatoes

1 small cauliflower

2 good sized tomatoes or a cupful of canned ones

2 hard-boiled eggs

1 teaspoonful of mixed herbs

1 oz. of butter

1 dessertspoonful of sago, pepper and salt to taste.

Wash all vegetables and prepare for cooking. Then cut each vegetable into pieces for the pie and set aside.

If you are using fresh tomatoes then scald them and once slightly cooled, remove the skin from them.

Combine all of the vegetables and let them cook together slowly in the butter and 1 pint of water. Let them cook until they are all tender.

Add in the herbs and seasoning for flavor and let it mix into the vegetables well.

Pour the mixture into a pie dish after cooked. Sprinkle with sago and then add more water if you want a gravy like consistency.

Cut up the hard boiled eggs into quarters and place these pieces atop the cooked vegetables. Cover it all with a crust to let cook together.

You can change up the vegetables to your taste and try options like legumes or beans as well. You may also substitute a pasta like vermicelle instead of the sago if you wish too.

Yorkshire Pudding

4 eggs

½ lb. of fine wheatmeal

1 pint of milk

pepper and salt to taste,

1 oz. of butter

Beat the eggs and then mix with flour and milk to make a batter. Season it for flavor with salt and pepper.

Butter the bottom of a dish and then pour in the batter. Cut up a little bit more butter and sprinkle over the batter to help bake to a golden brown.

Bake the mixture for about 45 minutes at 350, or until golden brown.

Serve hot and good with vegetables and potatoes. You may wish to serve with a simple sauce for extra flavor.

Macaroni/Pasta

Macaroni Cheese

½ lb. of macaroni

8 oz. of grated cheese

some breadcrumbs

pepper and salt to taste

1 oz. of butter

Bring macaroni to a boil in water, slightly salt the water just before it comes to a rapid boil. Cook macaroni until soft and then set aside after drained.

Take a scoop of cooked macaroni and lie it in the bottom of a pie dish to create a layer. Once bottom layer is complete, then add some of the grated cheese over the top of the macaroni.

Add salt and pepper over the top of the cheese layer. Then start over with a macaroni layer on top again and repeat the layering process.

End with a layer of cheese over the top of everything and then add the bread crumbs over the cheese.

Cut butter into pieces and then place atop the bread crumbs to allow this to melt and cook into the layers evenly.

Bake in the oven at 350 degress for about 30 minutes or until golden brown and butter melted nicely into the mixture.

Macaroni Cream

6 oz. of macaroni

3 oz. of cheese

½ oz. of butter

¾ pint of milk

1 teaspoonful of cornflour

pepper and salt to taste

Boil the macaroni according to package directions, ensuring you cook it until it is tender. Drin water out and set aside to mix in with other ingredients.

In the meantime make a sauce out of milk, cheese, and cornflour. Note that you can use several different kinds of cheese including Parmesan, Greyere, or Canadian cheese.

Once the sauce is created, this will go over the top of the macaroni while it is hot. Place macaroni in a pie dish and then pour the sauce over the top of it.

Place some grated cheese over the top of the macaroni with the sauce. Then place into a 350 degree oven and cook until golden brown. Serve hot.

Rice

Curried Rice and Tomatoes

½ lb. of Patna rice

1 dessertspoonful of curry powder

salt to taste

1 oz. of butter

Rinse the rice to prepare to cook.

Then mix rice, butter, curry powder, and salt together and let it cook together over a medium heat. Cover the rice and all of the ingredients and then let it all simmer until water is completely absorbed.

After about 20 minutes the water should be absorbed and then the rice will have the grains separated. This is how you want it to be for the final dish, so set it aside when complete.

For the tomatoes use the following ingredients:

1 lb. of tomatoes

a little butter

pepper and salt

Wash the tomatoes thoroughly and then place them into a dish with a bit of water.

Add some salt and pepper and small pieces of butter that you cut up over the top.

Bake all of this for about 15-20 minutes. Place the cooked rice into a dish and then add the tomatoes over the top, using any liquid that came out in cooking. Serve hot.

Savory Rice Croquettes

½ lb. of Patna rice

1-1/2 pints of milk

1 lb. of Spanish onions

1 oz. of butter

2 eggs

1 teacupful of raspings

's oil for frying

Place rice into milk and then boil until rice is tender. Then set aside once cooked thoroughly.

Chop onions finely and then sauté them in butter until they are tender and turn a light golden brown.

Take cooled rice and form into balls. With your thumb place an indentation in the middle of each rice ball. In this indentation, you will place a scoop of sautéd onions. Then close up the hole once the onions are in to form around it.

Dip each formed rice ball into beaten egg mixture and then raspings to coat them evenly.

Fry each coated rice ball in the oil until they are a light golden brown. Serve hot with gravy for a little extra flavor.

Omelets

Cheese Omelet

4 slices of bread that has been toasted or you can use an rusk.

3 eggs

¼ lb. of grated cheese

1 saltspoonful of nutmeg

1 pint of milk

2 oz. of butter

pepper and salt to taste

Beat eggs well and then mix with milk to create a nice mixture.

Crush the toast or rusks up with your hands for a nice crumble and texture. Then let this mixture soak in the egg and milk mixture.

After soaking, add the cheese, nutmeg, and other seasoning for taste and flavoring. Then let half of the butter dissolve and mix it in with all of the other ingredients.

Grease a pie dish with butter and then pour the complete mixture in. Sprinkle finely cut butter over the top of the mixture to let soak in during cooking process.

Bake everything together in the oven for about an hour at 350 degress. Should set well together and then can be served when hot or even cold.

Gardener's Omelet

1 cup of boiled vegetables now cold and minced fine (Try carrots, green peas
, turnips and potatoes)

4 eggs

1 tablespoon of fine wheatmeal

½ cup of milk

pepper and salt

a dash of nutmeg to taste

1 oz. of butter

Beat eggs thoroughly, and once complete then mix them together well with milk. This will form the foundation of the omelet so mix together well.

Add in the wheatmeal for texture, and allow this to mix well together. Then add in the vegetables and all of the seasoning to taste, including salt, pepper, and nutmeg.

Fry everything together as an omelet and let it cook until golden brown, and when everything is cooked together well.

Serve hot and enjoy!

Omelet Souffle

4 eggs

3 oz. of sifted castor sugar

the grated rind of ½ a lemon

1 oz. of butter

Beat yolks of the eggs together for about 10 minutes or until blended well. This will form the foundation of the souffle so take your time with this.

Add in sugar and lemon rind as you are beating the egg yolks.

Separately whip the egg whites until they come to a nice froth that is stiff in texture. Pour the entire mixture into a well greased pie dish.

Bake the souffle at about 350 degress for 10 to 15 minutes until golden brown.

Serve immediately out of oven when hot.

Omelet Tomato

1 lb. of tomatoes

½ lb. of breadcrumbs

1 large Spanish onion

3 eggs

2 oz. of butter

pepper and salt to taste

Chop onions up finely and then let them cook well in butter for about 20 minutes in a covered pan.

Chop tomatoes finely and then add to the onions, along with salt and pepper. Once cooked together, add onions and tomatoes to the remaining ingredients.

Let everything cook together for about 20 minutes over the stovetop.

Then add this to the breadcrumbs, pouring over the top of them. Add beaten eggs over the top of the mixture and mix everything together well.

Place mixed ingredients into a greased dish and then place into the oven at 350 degress for about 10-15 minutes.

Serve hot after removing rom oven.

Vegetables/Side Dishes

Celery (Italian)

2 heads of celery

½ pint of milk

1 oz. of butter

1 egg

1 cupful of breadcrumbs

pepper and salt to taste

Rinse celery and then chop into small pieces. Place into water and boil the celery for about 10 minutes.

Drain the celery and as it is cooling, place it into the pan with the milk, half of the butter, and salt and pepper for flavor. Let this all cook together gently until the celery is tender. Set aside to cool and let the flavors mix together well.

Beat the egg and put into the mixture as it is cooling. In the meantime grease a dish and then sprinkle breadcrumbs across the bottom as a layer.

Pour the celery mixture on top and place the remaining butter cut into small pieces on top evenly.

Bake everything together at 350 degress until it is golden brown. Serve hot.

Mushrooms (Stewed)

1 lb. of mushrooms

1 oz. of butter

½ pint of water

½ teaspoonful of herbs

½ saltspoonful of nutmeg, pepper and salt to taste

juice of ½ a lemon

the yolk of 1 egg

1 dessertspoonful of cornflour

Clean the mushrooms thoroughly using vinegar to really help. Then wipe them dry with a cloth and set aside.

Place butter, water, herbs, and seasoning into a pan and then add the mushrooms in. Stew the mushrooms like this for about 10-15 minutes until they are tender and well blended.

Use cornflour to thicken the mixture. Then add in the egg yolk and finally the lemon juice.

Once mixed together well, serve warm and enjoy.

Onions (Braised)

2 lbs. of onions

2 oz. of butter, vege-butter, or oil

pepper and salt to taste

Peel the onions and then slice lengthwise into thin but generous pieces. Add them to the butter in a pan and then sauté them until they are tender and golden brown.

Add water slowly to the mixture to create a gravy, then add in salt and pepper as this is cooking.

Let onions cook for about 20 minutes like this and then serve hot.

Egg Dishes

Apple Souffle

4 eggs

4 apples

2 oz. of castor sugar (or more if the apples are very sour)

1 gill of new milk or half milk and half cream

1 oz. of cornflour

the juice of 1 lemon

Wash apples, then pare them and cut them into small pieces. Let the apples stew with the lemon juice and sugar, allowing them to reduce to a pulp.

Beat the apple pulp that remains until smooth and return to pan.

Add milk to the cornflour and then add this into the apple mixture. Stir it frequently and then allow this to all cook together until it comes to a slow boil.

Set the mixture aside and allow it to cool.

Separate the yolks from the eggs and beat them separately. Then mix the beaten yolks into the apple mixture.

Whisk the remaining egg whites until they reach a stiffer froth like consistency. Then gently mix them in as the final ingredient into the apple mixture.

Pour the entire combined mixture into a greased souffle pan. Bake at 350 degrees for about 20 minutes or until golden brown. Serve immediately upon removing from the oven.

Curried Eggs

6 hard-boiled eggs

1 medium-sized English onion

1 cooking apple

1 teaspoonful of curry powder

1 dessertspoonful of fine wheatmeal

1 oz. of butter

salt to taste

Wash the apples and then chop them and the onions finely. Set the two of these into a pan with the butter and cook gently until they are golden brown.

Add about ½ pint of water and some salt to the mixture.

Combine curry and the wheatmeal with some cold water and use this mixture to thicken the sauce.

Allow everything to cook together for about 10 minutes until well blended. Then run this mixture though a sieve.

Take the sauce that you obtain from the sieve and return it to the pan. Add the eggs to the mixture and warm then in the sauce.

When all blended and cooked together well, serve hot and enjoy.

Egg and Tomato Sandwiches

4 egg

1 teacupful of canned tomatoes or ½ lb. fresh ones

pepper and salt

1 oz. of butter

Wash tomatoes if fresh. Scald the tomatoes and then skin them in preparation for cooking.

Place butter in pan and melt at a medium heat, then add in tomatoes. Cook tomatoes until they are tender and soft, and most of the liquid has evaporated.

Beat the eggs and then mix them into the tomatoes once they are cooled. Add in salt and pepper for flavor.

Mix together until blended well, then put aside mixture to cool in refridgerator. Top a favorite bread with the mixture for a delicious sandwich.

Egg Savory

6 hard-boiled eggs, shelled and sliced

in summer use 1 large breakfast cupful of boiled and chopped spinach

in winter Scotch kale prepared the same way

some very thin slices of bread and butter

nutmeg, pepper, and salt to tast

½ pint of milk

some butter

Grease a dish and place slices of bread and butter over the bottom to create a layer.

Then layer on top of the bread either some spinach or kale depending on what time of year you are preparing the dish.

Layer on top with sliced eggs. Then sprinkle nutmeg, salt, and pepper on top for flavor.

Repeat the layers and the over the final layer on top should be buttered bread. Finally pour the milk over the top of the mixture.

Cook in the oven at 350 degrees for 20-30 minutes until it is golden brown. Serve hot.

Eggs Au Gratin

3 hard-boiled eggs

1-1/2 oz. of grated cheese

1 oz. of butter

2 tablespoonfuls of breadcrumbs

a little nutmeg, and pepper and salt to taste

Once eggs are hardboiled and cooled, slice them and put them on the bottom of a greased dish.

Sprinkle cheese over the top of the hard boiled eggs. Then add nutmeg, salt, and pepper for flavoring.

Scatter breadcrumbs over the top and a bit of butter to help melt and turn golden brown upon baking.

Bake at 350 degrees for about 10 minutes, or until the top is golden brown.

French Eggs

6 hard-boiled eggs

½ pint of milk

1 oz. of butter

1 dessertspoonful of fine wheatmeal

1 dessertspoonful of finely chopped parsley

nutmeg, pepper, and salt to taste

Add butter and milk to a pan and bring to a slow boil. Add flour and a dash more cold milk upon boiling to thicken the mixture.

Add salt and pepper for flavor. Once the mixture is thickened put aside for a moment.

Cut hardboiled eggs into quarters lengthwise and place them into the thickened sauce.

Sprinkle parsley over the top for flavor and color. Serve warm with bread or toast for a nice meal.

Potato Souffle

2 oz. of butter

4 eggs

¼ lb. of castor sugar

½ oz. of ground almonds (half bitter and half sweet)

6 oz. of cold boiled and grated potatoes

1-1/2 oz. of sifted breadcrumbs

Stir butter in a dish well until it is creamed and smooth. Once soft and creamy, add egg yolks to the butter and mix well.

Then add in sugar and almonds. Beat the mixture for about 10 minutes.

Stir in breadcrumbs and potatoes and mix well. Finally add in egg whites that have been whipped to a stiff froth over the top.

Put mixture into well greased pan and bake at 350 degrees for about 45 minutes to an hour.

Serve hot.

Spinach Tortilla

4 eggs

1 oz. of butter

a teacupful of boiled chopped spinach

lemon juice

pepper and salt to taste

Wash spinach thoroughly and then squeeze some lemon juice over the top. Add salt and pepper to season.

Add to butter in a pan and then sauté the spinach gently until it is tender.

Beat eggs and add to the spinach once it is cooked. Mix together and let it set.

Turn the tortilla over a plate to set upside down. Serve hot.

Tarragon Eggs

4 hard-boiled eggs

½ pint white sauce

1 teaspoonful chopped tarragon

1 tablespoonful tarragon vinegar

2 yolks of eggs

Hard boil eggs and then once cooled slice them up. Lay sliced eggs into a greased dish.

Mix together tarragon and tarragon vinegar to white sauce and bring to a nice heat.

Once heated well, place the sauce over the top of the sliced eggs in dish.

Bake together at 350 degrees for 10 minutes. Serve hot with bread or toast.

Salads

Potato Salad

1 lb. of cold boiled potatoes

1 small beetroot

some spring onions

olives

4 tablespoonfuls of vinegar

2 of salad oil

a little tarragon vinegar

salt, pepper, and minced parsley

Cut the cold potatoes into small pieces and set aside in a bowl.

Cut up onions and olives finely and add to the potatoes.

Mix together vinegar, tarragon vinegar, oil, salt and pepper until they are blended well and there is a good flavor.

Pour this sauce over the top of the potatoes, olives, and onions. Toss gently to coat and blend all flavors together.

Once mixed well, garnish with parsley and beetroot.

Serve cold.

Summer Salad

1 large lettuce

1 head endive, mustard and cress, watercress

2 spring onions

2 tomatoes

two hard-boiled eggs

Finely chop the lettuce, endive, onions, tomatoes, and cress. Place all of these into a large salad bowl and then toss them together.

Add a mayonnaise based dressing over the top of the blend. Then top with slices of eggs and tomato slices. Garnish with cress for one final touch.

Serve cold.

Potato Dishes

Potato Cakes

3 fair-sized potatoes

1 egg

2 tablespoonfuls of fine wheatmeal

pepper and salt to taste

a pinch of nutmeg

Wash and peel the potatoes and then grate them into a bowl. Then set aside.

Beat the egg and then mix in with grated potatoes. Add flour and seasoning for flavor.

Mix everything together until blended well.

Heat butter or oil in a pan and then add potato mixture as pancakes and cook up until golden brown. Turn over and let cook on the other side.

Serve hot with sour cream and applesauce.

Potato Cheesecakes

1 lb. of mashed potatoes

4 oz. of grated cheese

1 oz. of butter

2 eggs

some bread raspings

2 tablespoonfuls of fine wheatmeal

½ a teaspoonful of mustard, pepper and salt to taste

Melt butter and then mix in with mashed potatoes until blended well. Then slowly add in cheese, flour, mustard, seasoning, and 1 well beaten egg.

Mix everything together until blended well. Gently form the mix into cakes and set aside on a dish.

Beat second egg in a bowl. Then dip each cake into this egg mixture, then dip into raspings.

Heat oil or butter in a pan and then fry up each dipped cake until golden brown. They will cook quickly, so keep over a medium heat and watch closely.

Serve hot with a good tomato sauce for extra flavor.

Potato Rolls

2 lbs. of cold mashed potatoes

1 boiled Spanish onion

1 oz. of butter

the yolk of 1 egg

a little nutmeg

pepper and salt to taste

and a teaspoonful of powdered thyme

Finely chop onion and mix with mashed potatoes.

Melt butter and then add to thyme and an egg yolk. Mix everything together well and then form them into balls that are about 3 inches long.

Brush each formed ball with oil or warmed butter over the top.

Flour the bottom of a dish and then place the brushed balls into the dish. Cook at 350 for about 10-20 minutes or until golden brown.

Serve hot and enjoy!

Potato Surprise

1 pint of mashed potatoes

1 oz. of butter

4 tomatoes

pepper and salt

1 tablespoonful of finely chopped parsley

Mix mashed potatoes with butter, then add salt and pepper for seasoning.

Grease each tin of a muffin pan and then create a layer out of the potato mixture in each cup.

Add a tomato into each cup. Then sprinkle with parsley, and finally season with salt and pepper.

Cover the top with another layer of the mashed potato mixture.

Cook in the oven at 350 degrees for a couple of minutes just until golden brown.

Potatoes (Curried)

6 good-sized potatoes parboiled

1 oz. of butter

1 teaspoonful of curry powder

¾ pint of milk

1 dessertspoonful of fine wheatmeal

Salt

lemon juice to taste

Wash potatoes and slice them. Place the potatoes into a pan and pour the milk over the top of them.

Add a touch of water to the curry powder, and then pour this over the top of the potatoes.

Finally add salt and butter to the mix and blend together.

Cook potatoes over the stovetop at a medium heat, let them get soft. When the potatoes are tender, add the meal to thicken the mix.

Add milk or water as necessary if the potatoes become too thick. Then let everything simmer at a medium heat for a couple of minutes.

Add lemon juice after complete and mix together. Serve hot.

Potatoes (Stuffed)

6 large potatoes

1-1/2 breakfast cupfuls of breadcrumbs

½ lb. of grated English onions

1 teaspoonful of powdered sage

1 ditto of finely chopped parsley

1 egg well beate

piece of butter the size of a walnut

pepper and salt to taste

Wash the potatoes thoroughly and then cut them in half.

Scoop the inside of the potatoes out. Be sure to leave about an inch of the outside of the potato on each side.

Mix all other ingredients together, adding just a touch of milk to ensure that this doesn't become too dry. You do want it to be solid and thick, but not too dry.

Fill each of the hollowed out potatoes with the mix, so that each shell is completely full.

Bake at 350 degrees for a few minutes until they are golden brown and cooked well together.

Serve hot.

Potatoes (Toasted)

Boil potatoes and then let them chill in refridgerator.

Cut up cold boiled potatoes into slices.

Brush the top of each potato slice with butter or oil.

Place each slice onto a grill or griddle to toast evenly through.

Only let each potato slice cook to a golden brown since they are already cooked. Get them to warm and brown,a nd then serve hot.

Cut cold boiled potatoes into slices, brush them over with oiled